Fire from the Heart 2025

Winners of the 2025 Muriel's Journey Poetry Prize

THREE OCEAN PRESS

Library and Archives Canada Cataloguing in Publication

Title: Fire from the heart, 2025 : winners of the 2025 Muriel's Journey Poetry Prize.
Other titles: Winners of the 2025 Muriel's Journey Poetry Prize
Identifiers: Canadiana 20250271109 | ISBN 9781988915579 (softcover)
Subjects: CSH: Canadian poetry (English)—21st century. | LCGFT: Poetry.
Classification: LCC PS8293.1 .F5793 2025 | DDC C811/.608—dc23

Editor: Kyle Hawke
Cover and Book Designer: Kyle Hawke
Front and back cover art: ©2024 James Picard

Three Ocean Press
Vancouver, BC
778.321.0636
info@threeoceanpress.com
www.threeoceanpress.com

First publication, October 2025

Muriel's Journey

When I first had the idea for this, I never dreamed that it would go on year after year. What a miracle. And we are now in another momentous year. 2020 was the beginning of the pandemic, and this year another terrible illness has shown itself, this time of a political nature. This is why I'm particularly grateful to our cover artist, James Picard, for showing the world that poets stand up against racism, homophobia, transphobia, ableism, violence, and all the other ills that are so loud now.

A thousand thanks to Kyle Hawke, who Dave Olson, one of our poets, called "the world's fastest editor" and who has once again pulled together this beautiful chapbook. Our judges this year were Mary Duffy, Michelle Poirier Brown, and Geneviève Wynand, and our first readers Donna Dykeman, Richard Sitoski, and Kyle Hawke. Their work is not easy; we get so many fabulous poems. Please read the judges' statement. Tova Mori continues to be helpful and eager to help with administrative matters. A big shoutout as well to Heart of the City and Word Vancouver, who continue to support us by inviting us to their events, as well as the Listening Post, our venue for our in-person event.

ISABELLA MORI, on the traditional, ancestral and unceded territory of the Sk̲wx̲wú7mesh (Squamish), Səlílwətaʔ/Selilwitulh (Tsleil-Waututh) and xʷməθkʷəy̓əm (Musqueam) Nations (Vancouver, BC, Canada)

The Muriel's Journey Poetry Prize

The Muriel's Journey Poetry Prize honours the vitality, vivacity, and outspoken presence of poet-activist Muriel Marjorie, who passed on in the fall of 2018. As an Indigenous social justice activist, poet, and spoken word artist, what Muriel had to say would often literally wake you up. Her enthusiastic encouragement of innovative creative endeavours was infectious.

The Muriel's Journey Poetry Prize is open to all residents of Canada and to Canadians living abroad. No submission fee is charged; instead, those entering are asked to provide a statement of their community involvement to demonstrate their active effort to improve the world around them. First prize is $100. The DTES prize is also $100 and celebrates poets with a deep connection to Vancouver's Downtown Eastside. Second prize is $50. Fortuna's Choice rewards one randomly selected poem with $35. Judges look for lively, outspoken texts that present ideas in unexpected ways.

For information on the Muriel's Journey Poetry Prize, please contact the organizers at poetryprize@murielsjourney.com or visit their Facebook page.

www.murielsjourney.com

All poems in this collection were submitted and subsequently were selected by judges as the winners of the sixth annual Muriel's Journey Poetry Prize.

Prizes were awarded at an online ceremony on September 14, 2025 as part of the Word Vancouver literary arts festival. The ceremony was hosted from the traditional and unceded territory of the Musqueam, Squamish, and Tsleil-Waututh peoples, but included winners reading from their home territories, as noted in their Community Involvement statements at the end of this book.

ORGANIZERS
Isabella Mori
Kyle Hawke

JUDGES
Mary Duffy
Michelle Poirier Brown
Geneviève Wynand

ABOUT MURIEL AND THE PRIZE

Muriel was a social justice activist, poet, and spoken word artist of Indigenous heritage from the Gitxsan nation's Owl Clan who spent a lot of time in the Downtown Eastside. In her work, she always explored new ways of expressing herself, always talked and wrote about what's urgent and important. Her energy was like fireworks and her hugs legendary.

Muriel died in November of 2018. At Muriel's memorial at the DTES' Listening Post, someone related that on her last day, Muriel said that while she was leaving, she was still continuing her journey. The text was accompanied by a picture of the sunrise on the day she died. Isabella was moved by this to do her part in Muriel's continued journey and decided to start a poetry prize in Muriel's honour.

Everyone liked Muriel. She encouraged creative people of all stripes to continue on their path of creativity and social justice. With the Muriel's Journey Poetry Prize, we hope to pass on inspiration and strength to all who create with a sense of justice in mind.

Because Muriel always did things a little differently, we're doing this poetry prize a little differently, too. Being keenly aware of how subjective the judging of poetry can be, we give a prize to a poet randomly selected from the longlist of those who met the entry requirement of "lively, outspoken ideas ... speak your mind and let the world know what you think ... look at your subject in an unexpected way ... take a risk in your composition ... be frank and unreserved." Another change is our 'entry fee', which consists of people showing how they contribute to their community. Lastly, we have two first prizes, a general one and one specifically for a poet with close ties to the Downtown Eastside.

Contents

Made of Holes
Jessica Lee McMillan

cherry petals falling on Pender Street's glass pipes, fall just the same
on Dr. Sun Yat-Sen's Chinese Garden with porous stones
harvested from the bed of Lake Tai.

on the free side, the rocks are concrete knock-offs
and girls duckface against the bamboo backdrop.
the gravel smells of piss and a bedraggled crooner
sing-coughs over the water.

yet the floating petals curve us all in the pond's warped mirror—
a community reflected among standing rocks
with our take-out bags, vape smoke through the holes of us:
petals, children weaving earth and moon gates.

we came here for something hallowed;
an unphotographable moment like when light enters
the shaded corners or when eyes meet on the street.

the pond reflects green in our sockets.
in its reflection we are the standing stones.

we have obvious holes.

we attempt cosmic joinery with sidewalk and shoe,
the tongue and groove of the garden roof in this oasis
sheltering us in a rough surround.

we are the stones with hole hearts
wanting to be holy and full.

Displaced
Ghia Aweida

Displaced are my people,
   whole families and loved ones
        with essential papers,
   identifications, and
        clothing they wore

exiled on foot
   walking for hours
        for days on end
   north of Palestine border
        into Lebanon

to settle in refugee camps
   sleeping in makeshift tents
        penniless
        homeless

hungry, thirsty, cold
   desperate for cleanliness
        a new shelter
        a safe home
        to call their own

waiting for work permits
   for months
   swallowing pride
        to earn a living
        working in jobs

 below skill levels
   poorly paid
   renting homes
   to keep body and soul
        thriving for more
   completing studies at night

receiving better employments
   better their incomes,
   schooling their children
         older children aiding
         to better household incomes

excluded from moral rights
   ripped off from under them
   since the day of exile
         slowly crumbling,
                  beneath the weight
                  of new government.

scattered throughout the earth
   identifications forever lost,
   original house keys in pockets,
         dreaming to return
         only to remain exiled
                  never able to return

their precious land and resources
   burned to the ground
   their agriculture uprooted
         thrown into bonfires,
         erasing their existence

building a new nation
   over the graves
   of their beloved ancestors
         who peacefully rested
         in old graves

where tombstones are now shattered
   forever stripped of their names
   of their identities
         and the culture they once knew.

My grandmother cut up my baby photos
Joel LeBlanc

My grandmother cut up my baby photos
and mailed the small, fragile pieces
back to mum after I was born.

I was told the story years later, when I
asked why we never saw her.

Noella had been too gentle for a harsh
Saskatoon farm, mum said.

A world of tractors, dead cows,
the wheatfields that slowly ate her.

Grandpa had turned bonecold
when the war got inside him,

and he couldn't handle
rages, tears, or mood swings,

so he sent her away to a hospital—
the sort where patients often

vanished into unmarked graves
behind the old building.

The doctors put electrodes on her
brain to burn away the ghosts,

they had to strap her down
while her body danced

like a medium
deep in her trance,

but at least she escaped
a frontal lobotomy.

When he brought her home
months later, bits were missing:

memories of names, faces, months,
the stitches she used for sewing,

and how to enjoy cooking
her husband's favourite meal,

it all crumbled away
like fingerbones.

I never met Noella, but
when I was eight she started

mailing Christmas ornaments
every year, just little things

for the tree: crafts and
baubles and stars,

with handwritten letters
asking about our lives,

as if the season stirred up
some old memory in her,

of when being gentle
didn't hurt.

FORTUNA'S CHOICE
The Evangelist
Katherine Koller

a young man slept on a metal bench in the sun
feet socked at the heels, toes exposed
face tucked in serene comfort

like the bent-headed contemplation
in a gilded copper medieval
miniature of Mark

writing gospel of loaves and fishes
and needle's eyes and riches
with half-bared feet

the young man's eyes suddenly opened
and smiled at me: holding your
ninety-three-year-old arm

hurrying away
from what the evangelist might say
in the golden light of the last day of summer

I think I'm a forest, pretending to be a person
Joel LeBlanc

I sold all my words to
the night-eyed antler queen,

in exchange for feet, hands, toes,
a body built for paying rent.

She cut off my tongue and
fed it to the mountain.

Now I go to work, smile
at customers, apologize

if they weren't satisfied
with their purchases,

would they like their receipt?

But I remember the taste of
graves, bones, teeth.

The dead slept in my throat,
and I was never sick

with small talk, with bills,

or wishing to still be
beautiful when I died.

A forest wants to be old,
to go crooked with age,

to feel the centipedes
crawling between its toes,

over

to hear the carousing of
drunk wood pigeons,

to have a belly fat and soft
with hot starlight.

Black Holes
Jessica Lee McMillan

the year I was born,
the first image of a black hole

but down here
concrete has been eating trees as visible proof

—this empty is dusty clutter—
and I relish the apple bin in the drugstore

between rat-trap malls, fight off a write-off day by drinking
the last blue light from the night sky

without thinking about the Disney vacuum
that sucks orbs of our facsimile wishes.

I'm seeing black holes everywhere:
in the patriarchy of Ursula's shell

—the device that sucks our voices
from our bodies—

and the pixels under Ariel's fins
that gulp oceans to cool machines that swish her tail.

yet things don't get simpler
near event horizon

and black holes don't erase my screen-glazed eyes
as my car idles on ancestor fuel—

they don't swallow the bottle's
tremendous gravity

or the poverty void chasing after me—
that last watery squirt of Pert Plus.

over

I'm looking for a patch
between pee holes burned in the grass

with a view through towers of echoing glass
in a place that is no place

where there is no black hole for today's news:
images of a destroyed city the same day another child is born.

Incomplete List of Things I'll Never Have to Do Again
E.A. Cockle

Feel lucky to have found a guy who doesn't call me gross for biting my nails
ragged, takes me from frozen pizzas to making dough from scratch, can
juggle while riding a unicycle.

Picture us as a family when you adopt my lab rat Priscilla after she learns
to activate the food pellet dispenser. You nicknamed her Prissy, printed a
tiny *Priscilla, Queen of the Desert* poster to stick on her cage.

Accept you drink because you're depressed—the doctor prescribed Prozac.

Scrutinize the DSM-IV for how we align when my psychology professor
warns, *Dating him will be hard for you.*

Drop the professor's class.

Gag down dregs in beer pitchers at ten minutes to closing, less concerned
about my rum-and-Coked bloodstream than protecting your liver.

Wonder why beer tastes like a mouthful of dirt punching the back of my
throat. My mom, craft brew connoisseur, assured me I'd develop a taste.

Avoid applying for the Paris semester and a summer program in Quebec.
My mom urged, *See the world.* I'd miss you too much.

Marvel at the five-hundred-year-old castle in Ireland we lived across the
street from. The stone tower used to be a prison, houses a wine museum.

Endure 24/7 bubbling from the wine-making kit you wanted for Christmas,
fermentation stench in every corner of our flat. The wine tasted like
turpentine mixed with grapefruit soda. You poured it in your morning
apple juice.

Ask myself WTF I was thinking buying you a wine-making kit.

over

Hurl pillows when you stagger in at 4:30 a.m., demand you sleep on the living room floor. Lie awake worrying you'll choke on vomit.

Learn from your boss at the Spaniard Inn that you down three pints of Guinness after a kitchen shift like they're cups of tea.

Find you pissed on my laptop while sleepwalking. Discover a panic attack feels like running a mile while standing locked in place.

Bite my nails to bloody stumps waiting to hear your key turn in the door— proof you haven't stumbled off the pier into the tide.

Lie awake so I can grab you if you get up.

Turn to Cosmopolitans to lull the mental looping of *What if no one ever loves me again?*

Think of you every time "Friday I'm In Love" by The Cure comes on. You said you fell in love with me on our first date, a Friday night, while those plinky guitar notes played.

Come home from the bar and tell you I need to leave.

Small Box of Cereal
Dave Thorvald Olson

Dad was a skim milk man
Specifically, powdered milk
Mixed with skim into a
Once-a-week concoction
Mixed into plastic juice jugs
With the slitted edge seen in every 1980s kitchen

Then slow cook the wheat berries overnight
With the milk for breakfast

School lunch peanut butter and jelly, not too much
Whatever fruit on the discount counter
Nights of sorting the "good enough"
Green grapes from trays bought for a dollar
Until never wanted to eat a grape

Wasn't a hostage of money
Not a lot and was a group of us
Kids
But like wasn't just saving for a rainy day
But hoping it would pour so he could use up
The dented cans of lima beans

He dehydrated with a car heater
And used a wheat grinder to show he was ready

When the rainy day finally came
There was nothing
Just
Investments to shady dealers from the church
And a sad face asking for dinner

I guess… I didn't really stop to watch
Choosing feigned abundance in my nothingness

over

Learning working less
Is the only goal
Time is everything
Time for art making
Looking, letter writing
Sexing, nothing

Anyhow, Mom made glittered candles
in a side hustle business to bring in extra money to
Use at her discretion which meant
Gilt-edged China dishes and festive gifts

Mantles and trees
That would look good when her mother and sister would come over

I became her diligent assistant
Decorating candles with peeled paper napkin designs
Melting wax, mod podge glue, rolling into glitter,
Dry, wrap with wax paper, pack into boxes
Off to Saturday markets
Never Sunday

At the market in New West(minster)
Was a lunch counter with formica curved counter
Stools on a swivel —
Except serving only breakfast because the market was mostly crafts
and mostly morning

When I'd go to help, we'd arrive early to set up the folding tables,

then

Before going to the table to sell
(gaudily yet intentionally crafted) decorated candles to strangers

Rush over to the diner corner before doors
Opened
And I'd choose one of those tiny
Boxes of cereal
The "brand name" ones,
Not the generics in a bulk bag

Carefully cut the box length once and width twice,
The wax liner into an "H"
Clumsy with a plastic butter knife
Fold open gingerly, crease slightly
And pour on a small carton
Of rare rich whole milk
And pleasantly briskly
Crunch away
Folding box just right for
The last of the cereal milk
Poured til tinted dripped

Onto my chin

FIRST PRIZE · HONOURABLE MENTION
Jessica Lee McMillan

Jessica Lee McMillan (she/her) is a poet and teacher with an English MA and creative writing certificate from SFU's The Writer's Studio. Her recent work has appeared/is appearing in *The Malahat Review*, *Crab Creek Review*, *CV2*, *QWERTY*, and *Canadian Literature*. She lives on the land of the Halkomelem-speaking Peoples (New Westminster, BC) with her little family and large dog.

   Jessica has been doing non-profit work for 18 years, including teaching at-risk youth, newcomers and refugees, and assisting people with multiple barriers get access to justice through front-line legal services. She is proud to be a civil servant and she finds purpose in amplifying voices.

SECOND PRIZE · HONOURABLE MENTION
Joel LeBlanc

Joel LeBlanc is an Acadian Canadian writer, poet, editor, reviewer, herbalist, and chef, currently living in Pōneke Wellington, Aotearoa, on Ngāti Pōneke land. His poetry has appeared in *Stone Circle*, *Takahē*, *Poetry NZ*, *Tarot*, *The Spinoff*, and more. During his weekends, when not writing, Joel spends time as a volunteer chef for Good Bitches Baking, providing baked goods and sweet Canadian treats for local community organizations.

DOWNTOWN EASTSIDE PRIZE
Ghia Aweida

The contestant is a Lebanese-born poet and writer of Palestinian origins. She takes her inspiration from rich Arabic poetry, English poetry, and other works. She now lives and resides in the Lower Mainland and is a member of the Downtown Eastside Writers, which stemmed after Thursdays Writers Collectives has closed. She is published in several anthologies, as well as published a few chapbooks and a full-length book. She is looking forward to publishing more books and winning first place in poetry in the near future. She lives and resides in Richmond, on the Musqueam 2 traditional, ancestral, and unceded territory.

FORTUNA'S CHOICE
Katherine Koller

I write for stage, screen, and page in Treaty 6 territory. Stage plays include *Coal Valley*, *The Seed Savers*, *Last Chance Leduc*, and *Riverkeeper*. Books are *Voices of the Land*, plays; *Art Lessons*, a novel; and *Winning Chance*, stories, winner of a High Plains Book Award; and *Earthen: Stories* (upcoming). My poetry has appeared in *Prairie Journal*, *NorthWord*, *Happiness Reflected*, *Funicular*, *The Lupine Review*, and online at *Poetry Pause*. I am a volunteer founding producer of Edmonton Script Salon, a monthly new play reading series since 2014. I once gave a free workshop on writing dialogue for DTES writers.

Honourable Mention
E.A. Cockle

E.A. Cockle is the author of a chapbook titled *Growing Up Skipper® Stands Up to the Haters*. She lives in Tkaronto (Toronto), where she works in sustainability communications, shops local passionately, and stocks Free Little Libraries in her neighbourhood to the best of her book-hoarding abilities. E.A. is proud to be part of the team launching the first-ever Toronto Climate Week in June 2026.

Honourable Mention
Dave Thorvald Olson

Former world rambler, now living on family ancestral land in the Setouchi bioregion of Japan, with footprints and (parts of) heart still on unceded Coast Salish lands. I contribute to communities by making & sharing stories through postal communiqué, zines, and spoken word — with an eye towards people living with chronic and complex illness, and mentoring youth with curiosity for creative arts. 'DaveO' curates a creative life archive at: daveostory.com #AlwaysBeKind

JUDGES' STATEMENT

Thank you, Isabella, for honouring us with the invitation to serve as judges. And thank you, poets, for trusting us with your words.

Through vivid imagery and language, the winning poems skillfully explore universal themes such as mental health and addiction, and community and displacement. Connection, in its myriad forms, is triumphant.

In order to give each piece the fullness of our care, we read the poems aloud to one another. We held and explored each submission with respect and curiosity. As well, we discussed and honoured the subjectivity that is inherent in the reading and evaluation of poetry. And in this incredible collection of work, the titles also received their due.

Each of us, as both reader and judge, felt invited into the poems and found that our own lived experiences became woven into our decision-making process. The many voices represented in this collection remind us that we, as Canadians, are a country of artists.

Mary Duffy
Michelle Poirier Brown
Geneviève Wynand

Judges' Biographies

Mary Duffy is a Vancouver children's and YA librarian. She is a longtime member of Pandora's Collective. Her poetry has been published in various journals and anthologies including *Quills*, *Leafpress*, *Blueprint Review*, *High Altitude Poetry*, *The Return of the Downtown Eastside Poets*, *The Soul of Vancouver*, and online at the *Globe and Mail*, as well as with *Telephone: An International Arts Project*. Her poetry comes from connection with community, whether that be in rural Newfoundland where she grew up or the poetry community. She currently lives and works on the unceded territories of the Musqueam, Squamish, and Tseil-Waututh nations.

Michelle Poirier Brown is a Métis writer, performer, and feminist activist. In 2022, she published *You Might Be Sorry You Read This* (University of Alberta Press) and *Intimacies* (JackPine Press) and was named a Writer to Watch by CBC Books. In 2021, Michelle's poem "A Cure for Sorrow, a Prescription for Despair" won second place in the Muriel's Journey Poetry Prize, and her poem "Before the Open Refrigerator Door" received an honourable mention. Michelle's poetry and short prose has been published in numerous literary journals as well as in over a dozen anthologies. Her essay "The Amnio Journal" received a 2021 *Malahat Review* nomination for a National Magazine Award in Personal Journalism. She lives in Vernon, in Syilx Okanagan territory.

Geneviève Wynand is a BC-based author, editor, writing coach, and presenter. Her words have appeared with *PRISM international*, *Grain*, *Tricycle*, and *Introvert, Dear*, among others. In her past life with Pulp Literature Press, she wore many hats, including acquisitions editor, line editor, and blog poster (semi-) extraordinaire. In the literary playground that she now calls home, Geneviève gets to host workshops, speak on panels, and offer blue-pencil and first-page sessions. Currently, she is co-writing a braided memoir/motivational book with her drum teacher, Ryan Van Poederooyen. Visit her at genevievewynand.com or on Instagram. @genevievewynand